W9-CPM-578

Farm Animals

by Tammy J. Schlepp

Copper Beech Books
Brookfield, Connecticut

Contents

© Aladdin Books Ltd 2000

Designed and produced by
Aladdin Books Ltd
28 Percy Street
London W1P 0LD

First published in the
United States in 2000 by
Copper Beech Books,
an imprint of
The Millbrook Press
2 Old New Milford Road
Brookfield, Connecticut 06804

ISBN 0-7613-1220-X

Printed in U.A.E.

All rights reserved

Coordinator
Jim Pipe

Design
Flick, Book Design and Graphics

Picture Research
Brian Hunter Smart

Cataloging-in-Publication data is on
file at the Library of Congress.

Come one! Come all!

Meet the animals that live on the farm.

Learn about the ducks and chickens.

Visit the turkeys and cows.

Welcome to the farm!

Farmyard

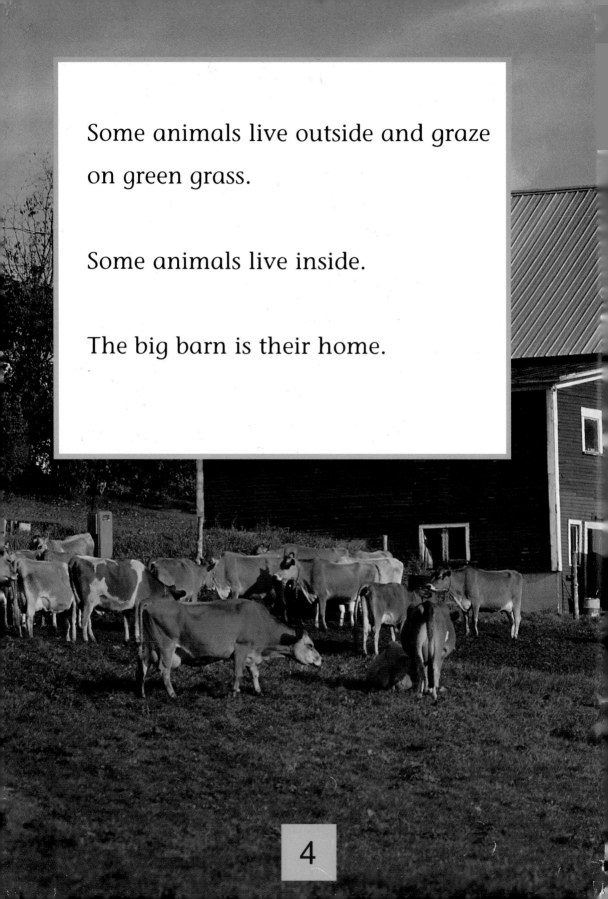

Some animals live outside and graze on green grass.

Some animals live inside.

The big barn is their home.

Farm

The red building is a barn.

Hi, my name is piglet and I squeal, "Oink, oink." I have a curly tail and a nose that's good for digging.

Piglets

My dinner is Mom's milk. See me eating with my brothers and sisters?

Yummy, yummy! I can't wait to fill my tummy.

Pig

Hello, my name is chick and I chirp,
"Cheep, cheep."

Hens

Rooster

I may grow up to be a
rooster and wake you in
the morning with my
"Cock-a-doodle-do."

I scratch the ground for seeds and worms
and eat them with my strong beak.
Yummy, yummy!
I can't wait to fill my tummy!

Chick

Turkey

Where is my beak?

Howdy, my name is turkey and I say, "Gobble, gobble." That red skin hanging from my beak is called a wattle. You may think of me at Thanksgiving.

Hi, I'm a duck and I say, "Quack, quack." My webbed feet help me swim. I dive for food with my tail in the air.

Ducks

Kids

Hello, we're baby goats and we bleat, "Maa, maa." Folks call us kids.

We can drink milk from a bottle like a hungry baby.

12

Howdy, I'm a little sheep and
I bleat, "Baa, baa."

I'm called a lamb.

A girl lamb is a ewe.
A boy lamb is a ram.

Lamb

Cows

Eating grass in a field.

I'm a dairy cow and I graze on grass.

My udders are full of milk for you to drink.

Two times each day I have to be milked.

Milking

I like to lie on the grass.

But at night I sleep standing up.

Cattle

You live in a house or apartment.

These cattle live on a ranch.

They live with other cattle in a herd.

16

Howdy, my name is bull, and I am big and tough. You need to watch out for my horns.

Bull

17

Our name is sheep.

From our old coats you may get your new wool coat. It doesn't hurt when the farmer cuts off our coats.

Sheep

My name is goat, and I have a beard under my chin.

I am nimble and quick and good at climbing too.

I can live on a steep mountain as well as on a farm.

Goats

Farmers like me because my milk makes good cheese for you to eat!

21

Hi, my name is sheep dog, and I bark, "Arf, arf." I'm the farmer's friend and helper.

Shepherd

Sheep dog

I keep the sheep flock together and protect them from wolves.

The farmer whistles at me to tell me what to do.

My name is horse, and I say, "Neigh, neigh."
When I was small, I was called a foal.

Horses

On ranches, I help round up cattle.

But most farmers keep me just for riding.

Pulling a plow

Hi! I'm a horse that helps the farmer. I pull a plow.

Howdy, I'm a water buffalo on a farm far away in Asia. I'm a hard worker in the muddy fields.

Water buffalo

26

Llama

Hi, I'm a llama from South America.

Farmers raise me for my woolly coat.
Get me angry and you may see me spit.

Can You Find?

Farm animals don't look like us.
They have horns and beaks and tails.

Can you find the farm animals to
match these parts?

Beak

Hoof

Snout

Foot

Tail

The answers are on page 32.

Clue: Look at pages 7, 9, 12, 17, and 25.

Horns

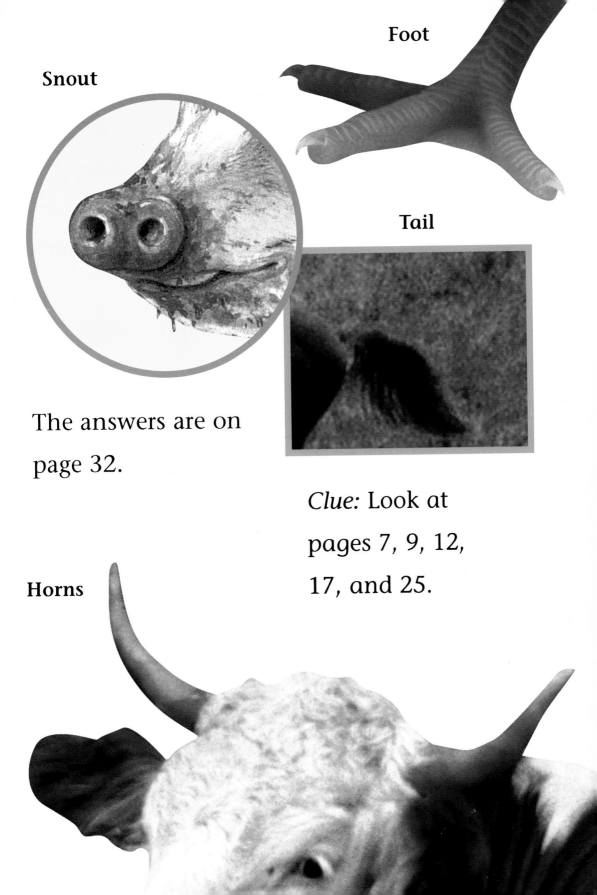

Do You Know?

Can you match the animals with
the things we get from them?

Llama

Sheep

Hen

Cow

Goats

Duck

Butter

Eggs

Wool
sweater

Milk

Cheese

The answers are
on page 32.

Index

ANSWERS TO QUESTIONS

Pages 28-29 – A chick has this **beak** • A goat has this **hoof** • A pig has this **snout** • A chick has this **foot** • A horse has this **tail** • A bull has these **horns**.

Pages 30-31 – We get **butter** from cows • We get **eggs** from hens and ducks • We get **wool** from sheep and llamas • We get **milk** and **cheese** from cows, sheep, and goats.

Photocredits: Abbreviations: t-top, m-middle, b-bottom, r-right, l-left, center. Cover, 2, 9, 10, 14, 28bl, 29t—Stockbyte. 1, 12, 17, 28m, 29b, 30mr, 30bl—John Foxx Images. 3, 11, 13, 31 all—Select Pictures. 4-5, 6, 8, 16, 18t, 18-19, 22, 26 both, 27, 30t, 30ml—Corbis Images. 15—Christine Osborne/Corbis. 20-21, 24-25, 29mr, 30c, 30br—Digital Stock.
Illustrators: Wayne Ford—Wildlife Art Ltd.